THE
TUTORIAL
PROCESS

by

Howard S. Barrows

Southern Illinois University

School of Medicine

Revised Ed
D1141984

Published by
Southern Illinois University School of Medicine
Springfield, Illinois

ISBN - 0-931369-25-8
Library of Congress (92-085427)
First Edition published 1988
Revised Edition published 1992

Table of Contents

NOTE

The author has enjoyed working with excellent tutors and students of both genders throughout his teaching career; however, for the convenience (or elegance) of style, the male pronoun will be used in this book.

BACKGROUND

Although the term "tutor" may not be ideal for a teacher employing a facilitatory or maieutic teaching style, it has become commonly used in this way. The ability of the tutor to use facilitatory teaching skills during the small group learning process is the major determinant of the quality and the success of any educational method aimed at 1) developing students' thinking or reasoning skills (problem solving, metacognition, critical thinking) as they learn, and 2) helping them to become independent, self-directed learners (learning to learn, learning management). Tutoring is a teaching skill central to problem-based, self-directed learning. (Barrows and Tamblyn 1980, Barrows 1985).

Although tutorial teaching seems natural for some teachers, it is a difficult skill to understand and apply for many teachers who are used to didactic teaching approaches. The intent of this handbook is to present a conceptual basis for facilitatory teaching skills that may make them easier to understand, practice and develop.

Attempts to define this teaching role usually concentrate on what the tutor should not do. He is told that he should not put students into a passive learning role by giving them the facts they need or by lecturing to them; students should actively acquire the facts they need on their own. The tutor is also told that he should not tell his students whether their ideas presented in discussions or their answers to questions are right or wrong; they should find out for themselves, under the tutor's guidance. Descriptions of what the tutor should do are less specific and usually difficult to understand. He is told that the tutor should facilitate or guide learning by encouraging students to present and discuss their own ideas and to determine their own learning needs. The usual result is that the new tutor will either sit in the group and say nothing or will try to encourage student discussion in a non-specific way.   Unsure of what to say or how to facilitate learning, he characteristically falls back on the more comfortable and understandable direct teaching or didactic style when students seem to be wandering off course, expressing incorrect information or ignoring important facts and concepts.

The tutorial style associated with the case method of teaching and often seen in movies and television has been analyzed by Collins and Stevens (1983). This teaching style is often confused with the facilitatory tutorial method used in small groups that will be described here. Although the case method teacher does not directly give information to students but challenges them to present their own thinking, he does provide them with information and direction. The case method teacher does this by responding to the students' ideas with counterexamples, absurdities that would result from their ideas, data not explained by their ideas, or by providing them with new facts that will shape their thinking at a critical point. Although the students are required to think and to defend their ideas in the case method, they will usually know from the teacher's responses if they are right or wrong. In the case method, the students are certainly challenged to reason and learn on their own and are not as dependent on the teacher as in more didactic, lecture approaches; but they are not as independent of the teacher as in the facilitatory tutoring method described here. In this method, students learn to become self-reliant and eventually independent of the tutor. This method is particularly important in the education of professionals (medicine, business, law, engineering, social work, etc.) where students are eventually expected to become independent, problem solving, self-motivated learners.

THE TUTOR FUNCTIONS AT THE METACOGNITIVE LEVEL

F ew problems or situations in everyday life or in professional practice present themselves with all the information that is needed to understand them well enough to make valid decisions about their cause and their resolution; more information is needed.

Some of the needed information is obtained by investigating the problem, making observations, asking questions, testing and probing (history, physical examinations and laboratory tests in medicine, for example). To determine what inquiries, observations, or investigations should be made requires reflection, thought and deliberation.

Some of the information needed to understand the problem or situation has to come from knowledge in the memory of the problem solver; recalled facts, concepts and prior experiences relevant to the problem. A portion of this information in memory may come to mind automatically, cued by memory associations with familiar elements of the problem encountered. Recalling the rest requires reflection, review, thought and deliberation. These words; thought, reflection and deliberation, represent aspects of what will be described below as "metacognition."

External information, beyond the problem solver's own knowledge or expertise, may be needed to enlarge upon, correct, or sharpen the internal information in memory. This is especially true of new, unexpected, unusual or complex problems. Even the experienced expert rarely finds two problems that are the same. External information resources are wide and varied; records, books, journals, technical reports, automated information retrieval systems, and persons knowledgeable about various aspects of the situation or problem (experts, teachers, consultants and colleagues). To decide on what external information resource is needed and where and how it might best be found again requires deliberation and reflection.

As the problem is being probed and examined through inquiry, new information is obtained - information beyond that initially available when the problem or situation was first encountered. This new information often causes the perceived nature and extent of the problem to change, as there may be new ramifications and twists to the problem not anticipated at the outset. As before, these have to be pondered, deliberated and reflected upon.

Despite careful problem inquiry and analysis, and the accumulation of appropriate internal and external information about the problem, it is often the case that all the information needed to make the problem totally understandable and its proper solution or resolution obvious, is not available. Also, some of the information that was obtained may be confusing, conflicting or ambiguous. At some point, the problem solver has to make decisions and carry out actions on the basis of probability or intuition; and that takes more thinking, review, reflection and deliberation.

These are steps taken by good problem solvers, professionals, or experts.   These steps may be performed rapidly and almost unconsciously, often with shortcuts, by the problem solver who has accumulated considerable experience and knowledge from the kinds of problems he deals with daily. However, when the experienced expert runs across an unfamiliar, complex, confusing or difficult problem, all these steps become apparent as does the metacognitive effort required. In the town where you live, you can drive downtown to just the place you want with little thought, using known and effective shortcuts. However, in a strange town or a town you have been in only occasionally, the problem of finding your way will require observations and probes, what internal information you might have in memory and often external sources such as other persons and maps. The unfamiliar, unusual, new and perplexing problem or situation requires deliberation, reflection, review - or metacognition.

Metacognition is this executive function in thinking: pondering, deliberating, or reflecting on the problem or situation; reviewing what is known and remembered about the kind of problem confronted; creating hypotheses; making decisions about what observations, questions or probes need to be made; questioning the meaning of new information obtained from inquiry; pondering about other sources of information; reflecting on and reviewing what has been learned, what it all may mean and what needs to be done next, etc. Anyone who does not use metacognitive skills when faced with a difficult problem is an impulsive thinker, someone who operates on reflex behaviors, guesses or hunches (i.e. without thinking). This is the student we all dread and the professional from whom we would prefer not to receive a service.

Students must acquire, through practice, well developed metacognitive skills to monitor, critique and direct the development of their reasoning skills as they work with life's ill-structured problems; to critique the adequacy of their knowledge and to direct their own continued learning.

This concept of metacognitive thinking skills provides the key to the positive, active role of the tutor. Metacognitive skills are thinking about thinking. They are used when one is confronted with a difficult, unexpected or puzzling problem or situation. It is the conscious monitoring and directing of problem solving or reasoning activities. Schon (1983) has described the metacognitive problem solving activities of a variety of professionals as "reflection in action." He refers to these skills as a conversation with a problem.

When confronted with a difficult, unexpected or puzzling situation or problem, the problem solver must ask himself questions such as "What is going on here?" "Do I have the entire picture?" "Have I thought of all the possibilities?" "What data do I need to consider such possibilities?" "Do I have all the facts needed?" "What does this finding mean?" "What is the best way to manage this?" "Have I had experiences with situations such as this in the past?" "Am I right about this or is there another way of looking at it?" "Do I know enough about this kind of thing?" "What facts do I need?" "Where can I find them?" etc. etc.

To become independent of the tutor, to develop the ability to solve problems and to be able to learn on their own the rest of their lives, students must not be put into passive learning situations where the tutor determines what should be learned, to what depth, and in what sequence. Instead, students should be able to practice dealing with problems and learn to identify what they need to learn in that process. They should determine the proper resources for their learning and subsequently apply what they learned to the problem - under the **guidance** of the teacher as a tutor. To facilitate student independence and foster students' critical thinking and self-directed, continued learning, the tutor should guide his students at the metacognitive level. The oral statements and challenges he makes should be those he would make to himself when deliberating over such a problem or situation as the one his students are working with. His questions will give them an awareness of what questions they should be asking themselves as they tackle the problem and an appreciation of what they will need to learn. In this way he does not give them information or indicate whether they are right or wrong in their thinking. This is the intent of this metacognitive modeling by the tutor; to initially guide the students in their thinking and to stimulate them to adopt similar metacognitive skills on their own; to be reflective, carefully reasoning thinkers and not impulsive ones. He interacts with them at this level until they naturally and automatically develop the habit of challenging each other with similar questions at the metacognitive level. In this way, deliberate, reflective, thoughtful thinking becomes a group habit through practice. The desired end point is when each student employs his own metacognitive skills automatically and easily with every task, situation or problem. Good tutors know that if they are successful, the tutorial group will eventually run on its own. The students should become independent problem solvers and self-directed learners. As will be discussed later, modeling, coaching and then fading away are part of the architecture of the tutorial process.

This interaction at the metacognitive level is the basic function of the tutor. Using this approach, the tutor can make certain that students do not wander off too far in wrong or non-productive directions and that they meet important curricular objectives with the problem they are working with. When properly done, this guidance is not apparent to the students, as they think they are in charge of the learning process. For example, if students have not entertained the correct hypothesis as to the underlying mechanism for a problem, the tutor can always ask, "Are there other possibilities that you may not have thought of?" Or if a new finding makes the correct hypothesis more obvious, he could say, "Let's stop and review our hypotheses again." If a student expresses a completely incorrect idea, the tutor can turn to others in the group and say, "Do you agree with that?" or "What is the supporting evidence for that idea?" However, this maneuver will certainly be transparent if the tutor does not also say similar things when students are correct in their statements or reasoning. As this guidance is covert and the students are unaware that it is going on, they think that the thinking that went on in the group, the path they followed in their reasoning, and the learning issues they identified were solely of their own doing. This makes students feel as though they are responsible for their own learning, as they eventually must become in this tutorial process.

The structure, or architecture (see later), of educational and tutorial processes and the stages that occur in reasoning through a problem can provide the tutor with a road map for the sequence of metacognitive questions that should be asked of his students. The same process is used to shape students' self-directed learning and the subsequent application of newly learned information to the problem.

ADDITIONAL TUTORIAL TASKS REQUIRING FOCUSED QUESTIONS

There are a number of additional tasks for the tutor that are essential for a small group's learning process. Some were mentioned in the previous description of the tutor's metacognitive tasks. Some of these additional tasks can also be carried out with questions aimed at the metacognitive level. The timing of these tasks during the group process is important.

The first task is to **keep the learning process moving, to make sure that no phase of the learning process is passed over or neglected and that each phase is taken in the right sequence.** If the students are to reason their way through a problem, the tutor must be certain that the students exercise their reasoning and apply the information they already have stored in their minds at every stage in the problem solving or reasoning process. For example, the tutor should be certain that he explores all possible hypotheses or explanations for the **cause** of the problem before allowing the group to go on to an inquiry to gain more information about the problem. If self-directed study is important to the group's learning process, the tutor must be certain that the students recognize any doubts they may have about the correctness or sufficiency of the information they now possess and that they note down the information they should seek as learning issues they will need to pursue. The identifiable stages in the reasoning process, or self-directed learning process, each represent logical points for deliberation and reflection before moving to the next. The whole sequence of stages that needs to be considered by the tutor using problem-based, self-directed learning can be outlined (Barrows 1985) and represents one aspect of the architecture of the process described below. (See Appendix I) Later, other reasoning processes will be discussed.

The second task is to **probe the student's knowledge deeply**. To do this, the tutor must constantly ask "Why?" "What do you mean?" "What does that mean?" "How do you know that's true?" -- again and again until the student has gotten down to the depth of understanding and knowledge expected of him and has brought out all he knows (often more than he realizes he knows). The tutor must **never** let ideas, terms, explanations or comments go unchallenged or undefined, "What do you mean by that, tell us what you know?" "Would you explain that?" Anytime a scientific term, label or eponym is used, the student should be asked to define the term. You cannot assume that a student correctly understands a concept or entity because he can use the label correctly.

For example, whenever a student wants to ask a question of the patient whose problem is being analyzed by the group, or whenever a student wants certain information about a problem the group is dealing with, the tutor should ask, "Why do you want to know that?" Invariably, that student will reveal a hypothesis or idea that he was harboring in his mind about the cause of the problem; a hypothesis or idea he might not have otherwise ever mentioned in the group. Thinking must be probed. The tutor must find out what internal metacognitive ideas drive the external activities of the students. When a student learns/gains the information he was looking for or the patient's answer to his question, the tutor should ask, "What did that do for you, what does it mean in terms of your idea about the problem?" There is a tendency for tutorial groups to remain superficial in their discussions and to use terms and concepts without having to dig to deeper levels to answer why, what, where and when. The tutor has got to probe for deeper, more fuller explanations and descriptions of phenomena at a more basic level.

It is the failure of the tutor to push the students down to the depth of understanding required that has prevented many teachers from appreciating that this kind of learning can lead to the depth of knowledge they feel the student must achieve in more didactic approaches. After the tutor has probed in this manner enough times, the students will almost automatically begin to inquire and learn at a deeper level of understanding.

The third task is to be sure that **all students are involved in the group process.** When one student expresses an idea or an opinion, the tutor needs to be sure others make whatever comments they may have, that different opinions or points of view are heard. He needs to get group discussion and consensus on most issues and ideas. When, for example, hypotheses concerning the causes of a problem are being sought, all students should have an opportunity to express their ideas and each should be able to comment on the ideas of the others. This prevents students from withdrawing from the group and prevents assertive students from always running the show. It also allows the tutor to monitor the progress of each student in the group. (See "educational diagnosis" in the next section).

To facilitate student exchanges, the tutor has to be sure that he gets out from being the center of all discussions. If he is not careful, he will find that each student is answering only his questions and that each student is addressing him in the discussions and not each other. Instead of a working group, you have five or six individuals, each interacting with the tutor. This can be avoided by using several strategies. When a student addresses the tutor with a statement or question, the tutor can say, "Who has some thoughts about this comment (or question)?" When a student addresses the tutor or responds to one of the tutor's questions looking directly at the tutor, another strategy is for the tutor not to answer; just to wait and see if other students will get involved. A useful variation of this latter strategy is for the tutor not to answer and, in addition, turn and look at another student as if the tutor is expecting that student to answer. It helps if the tutor does not sit in the center of the group where students are bound to face him. He should sit at the corner of the table so the students face each other and he can lean back and get out of the group if it seems to be running on its own power. When the group members begin to carry on active discussions between themselves, the tutor should physically take his chair and back out of the group's line of sight.

Another task for the tutor is **educational diagnosis**. He should continually monitor the educational progress of each student in the group. Early recognition of any learning difficulties such as reasoning difficulties, difficulties in understanding the information and concepts discussed by the group, or problems in finding appropriate information through self-directed study (to cite only a few common problems) is necessary to allow for early educational intervention and help. This is one of the greatest advantages of the small tutorial group; the tutor can assist students with educational difficulties and students can help each other. Help can be given before the student has to move on to new areas, poorly understanding what should have been learned thus far; or the student has gotten so far behind, or frustrated in trying to catch up, that continued learning is progressively more difficult. This last can be a vicious cycle. The student has only a weak foundation of knowledge and understanding on which to build; his attempts to catch up are therefore seriously undermined, resulting in further slippage, and more frustration; at this point the time that needs to be devoted to further efforts at catching up has become unrealistic. Basic information and concepts have to be fully comprehended before higher learning can be assimilated. The final examination is not the time to find out about a poorly performing student; by then it is too late. The learning issues assigned to a student in difficulty with certain concepts can be tailormade to help him understand the difficult area with further assistance from students in the group.

Focused metacognitive questions can be used as an inquiry tool by the tutor. He can challenge a student in an area in which he may suspect the student is having difficulty. This is applying the model of clinical diagnosis to educational diagnosis, as the teacher inquires through questions at a metacognitive level about suspected learning problems. For example, if a student returns to the group with inadequately researched information, the tutor may begin to gently probe the student's knowledge to determine its true depth and extent. If he feels that the student's replies are confused, vague or inadequate, he might ask "How do you feel about those facts you brought to the group today?" or, "Were you able to find all the resources you wanted?" When a student seems to have difficulty reasoning, the tutor can ask, "Are you comfortable with the way you have put that together?" etc. Asking other students to comment on what seems like an inadequate response by a student may also help.

The best outcome is that, as a result, the student himself sees and admits to an inadequacy in his learning or reasoning, and a plan can be made for remediation. For this to work, there is that cardinal rule, already mentioned, that all students must receive challenges about their thinking, or to the statements they make, when the tutor thinks they are **right** as often as when he feels that they are **wrong**. In this way such questions will be regarded as the norm by students when, in fact, they may be focused, diagnostic questions for a particular student. As in all tutorial activity, it is hoped that the students will eventually begin asking each other and, ultimately, themselves such questions when they perceive that there is a learning difficulty. Then the tutor is not needed to help the group or the individual student to perceive educational problems. The treatment of educational problems can be handled as a group process; suggestions from the group for study approaches or materials, students coaching students, the use of educational experts on the faculty, etc.

In a similar vein, the tutor can aim questions at students who seem not to be contributing to the group's ongoing discussions. As mentioned previously, it is important for the tutor to make sure that all the students contribute to the group's deliberations and express their own ideas and knowledge. Otherwise neither the student nor the tutor will know how students are progressing and whether knowledge and thinking skills are sufficient. The non-participating students must be drawn into the conversations by questions aimed directly at them. It is too easy to become involved with the talkative students and ignore the quiet one. The tutor has to watch all students all the time and ask himself how each is progressing in the learning process.

A last, but very important task is to **modulate the challenge of the problem or task at hand**. This is a key to successful learning. The students should not be bored by a learning process that moves too slowly or covers ground that is too easy. Boredom inhibits learning and the desire or inner drive to learn. At the other end of the scale, the task faced by the students should not be so large and complex that there is just too much to be learned and students become overwhelmed, frustrated and burned out. Attention and the drive to learn suffers along with the enjoyment and excitement of learning. The tutor must steer a course in between with the challenge of his metacognitive questions. He can ask, "Why?" "What do you mean?" "What is the evidence?" "Are there other explanations?" "Have you thought of everything that needs to be considered?" "What's the meaning of that?" etc. to crank up tension and interest. To decrease the challenge, he can ask questions such as "Should we just tackle a piece of this problem (or task)?" "Let's revise our objectives and tackle those that are most important in this task." "Maybe we ought to stop here and read some resources or go talk to an expert?" "Would it be better to get the big picture now and fill in the details later?" etc. A good term for this role of the tutor is "creative tension."

The motivation that comes from within the student to understand the problem, to gain the knowledge needed, is another of the great assets of small group learning. Motivation enhances learning and retention. Motivation is maximized by the tutor's vigilance in keeping up the challenge always there, but avoiding overload.

MANAGING INTERPERSONAL DYNAMICS, ANOTHER TUTORIAL FUNCTION

A nother skill expected of the tutor working with a small group of students is an ability to help the student group deal with their own problems of interpersonal dynamics. Interpersonal problems inevitably arise in any tutorial group and can inhibit its effectiveness. This skill is a requirement for the leaders of any type of small group.

When student groups first get together, everyone is on his best behavior; interpersonal problems usually do not surface until students and tutor have gotten used to each other and let their guards down. Eventually, differences, individual behaviors, habits, values, opinions, and desires become less tolerable once the group knows each other. This may take three to four weeks. The tutor needs to be sensitive to cues of disharmony or ineffectiveness in the group. Silence, late arrival, sarcasm, lack of individual productivity, lack of spontaneity, arguments in the place of relaxed discussions, students taking sides on an issue, expressions of dissatisfaction with learning or attempts by a student to take over in the group are all symptoms. A most common symptom, often not recognized, is a lack of progress in the group's tasks - things get bogged down because they cannot agree on where to go with a problem or task, or spend a long time on cyclic or trivial discussions. An awareness of the possibility that these kinds of problems may surface at any time is a key to managing these problems. The earlier they are recognized, the more effectively and promptly they can be handled.

The tutor should not take on a parental or fully responsible role in dealing with these interpersonal problems when they occur. This will make the students dependent on him and they will expect him to solve them. The students must learn to deal with interpersonal dynamics throughout their professional careers as they will inevitably have to work with people with whom they may not naturally get along well.

When interpersonal problems become apparent to the tutor in the ongoing activity of the group, the approach is best aimed at the metacognitive level. The first important issue is how to get the group itself or any student in the group to recognize that there is a problem. Ideally, the tutor ought to let the problem go long enough for a student eventually to express a concern that there is a problem or that the group does not seem to be going anywhere or accomplishing anything. The tutor's metacognitively tuned responses would be, in effect, "What do you suppose is going on?" - and later - "What shall we do about it?" etc.

Oftentimes the tutor cannot let the group deteriorate while he waits for someone to say something. Early in the group process he may have to set the example for problem recognition by modeling the behavior he hopes the students will acquire and say, for example, "There seems to be something going on here between us in this group," or, nodding to a particular student, "Why are you behaving this way?" or "We seem to be going nowhere as a group."

If the ensuing discussions cannot resolve the problem, then the group has to get the issues involved in their behaviors and the feelings behind them, out on the table and design a way to manage them. The tutor can suggest that the group considers itself and its interpersonal problem(s) as the next item to be tackled by the group in its studies. This can be accomplished in an evening or on a weekend, at someone's home. Here the discussions can be open-ended and last as long as necessary to get them resolved. In this process, it should be made clear that the members of the group do not have to like each other, but they do have to learn to work together effectively. Once these inevitable interpersonal dynamic problems are resolved, most groups become very efficient and productive.

Attending to the group's educational progress at the metacognitive level and the group's interpersonal dynamics, are the two basic challenges of the tutor in small group learning. If the tutor appreciates that he is the student's metacognitive conscience, his specific teaching role should be more understandable. This understanding allows the tutor to question the students and respond to their interactions in a way that is natural for him and his own particular personality. Instead of trying to memorize or mimic the questions tutors are supposed to ask, the tutor can guide the students and their progress expressing metacognitive thoughts in his own way.

THE ARCHITECTURE OF THE SMALL GROUP PROCESS

The next consideration for the design of the tutorial process in small group learning is the architecture or overall structure necessary to accomplish the learning tasks of the group. How should the group process begin and how should it end? What sequences of activity between tutor and students should go on between?

This architecture has three dimensions. The first dimension is the **sequence of reasoning (problem solving) and learning tasks** or behaviors that are appropriate for the task, situation or problem presented to the students. In problem-based learning, the problem is usually undertaken first to allow the students to see how far their present knowledge and reasoning skills can take them; to allow them to recognize, within the constraints of the curricular goals they will need to learn, what resources they will need to use to acquire the information needed. In the sequence of problem-based learning, the next small group session occurs after the students have carried out what they deem is appropriate self-directed study and return to the group to apply what they have learned to the task or problem, and then synthesize and evaluate what they have learned. This sequence is designed to take full advantage of small group learning. (See Appendix I) If instead, the group has to do such things as analyze a written case, critique an artistic work, design a social plan, solve a mathematical or physics problem, the sequence of activities in this architecture for the learning process may take another form. This architecture, the sequence of teaching/learning events, should be designed ahead of time.

The second architectural dimension is the **sequence of changes in the tutor's role in relationship to the students' roles.** Collins, Brown and Newman (Collins et al. in press) divide the tutorial role into three phases: modeling, coaching, and fading. In the beginning sessions of the group, the tutor applies his metacognitive challenges frequently, making certain that the students carefully consider each step in their reasoning, their learning needs and also identify learning resources, etc. He is **modeling** the thinking process for his students, demonstrating to them the questions that should be asked to deal with the problem or task at hand.

As the group becomes comfortable and adept at the process, the tutor interjects his challenges only when the students may miss a step in the process, seem to be wandering, or are confused. This guidance can be considered **coaching.** As the students progress, the tutor deliberately and progressively withdraws or **fades**, eventually leaving the students on their own.

Therefore, in the beginning of the tutorial group sessions, the tutor will often have to be more direct and demonstrate the cognitive problem solving behaviors eventually expected of the student and to be more directive about learning issues and resources for self-directed study. Keeping this modeling-coaching-fading architectural dimension in mind helps remind the tutor that he should eventually become unnecessary to the group.

The second phase, coaching, is seen when the students become more proficient in their own reasoning and the tutor has to interject only occasionally when the students are stuck or have deviated in their process. Collins (1983) offers the term "scaffolding;" when the tutor provides a support structure to guide the students at a less direct level.

The third architectural dimension is **the change in the group's interpersonal behavior over time**. As mentioned previously, at the outset all are on their best behavior, courteous, friendly, and accommodating. Each member holds back any irritations, frustrations and strong personal opinions he may have when among strangers. It varies, but usually after three weeks or so, the natural vexations that occur between persons working together intensely, no longer strangers, or vexations with the activities of the group that may not suit some of the students, begin to surface in a variety of ways. Arguments between students, withdrawal from the group, students attempting to take over the group, expressions of discomfort and many more behaviors are, as mentioned previously, a signal to the tutor that the group will need to take on its own behavior as the next problem. Once these interpersonal issues have been resolved, the next phase is usually one of high output and productivity. The last phase, when the group knows that its time has come to break up as the course will end soon, has been referred to as the group's "death and dying" phase. The students frequently attempt to make arrangements to get together and keep in touch - even to continue to meet, with or without the tutor.

An awareness of these phases in the overall architecture of the group's interpersonal progress helps the tutor understand what and where the group is going and not to be distressed by the inevitable group dysfunctions that occur even in the best of groups with the best of tutors. This architecture underlines the fact that it is inappropriate to have small tutorial groups function for less than eight to ten weeks. In a shorter period of time students may never really get comfortable with the small group learning process or with each other, and thus never reap the rewards of the high output phase.

REVIEW OF THE GENERAL PRINCIPLES FOR TUTORIAL TEACHING

In the beginning, these principles may not be employed fully as the tutor attempts to move the students into a learning independence. Initially, the tutor may have to give some information and direction, express an opinion, suggest what the students ought to do next. However, the tutor must ensure that these principles are progressively employed.

1) The tutor's interactions with the students should be at a metacognitive level, except for interactions that concern "housekeeping" activities (schedules, places to meet, orientation activities, announcements).

2) The tutor must carefully guide the students through all the steps of the particular learning process required. If an ill-structured problem or situation is to be analyzed or evaluated, the tutor must be sure the students go through all the stages of the hypothetico-deductive process. If a case or report is to be studied, the tutor should carefully guide students through analysis and synthesis. If action steps or solutions of a problem are to be undertaken, the students must entertain alternatives and consider pros and cons, etc. The tutor should be certain that each step in whatever process is appropriate, is thoroughly covered.

3) The tutor must push the student to a deeper level of understanding and bring out the knowledge that is embedded in the student's mind by the use of constant, almost irritating probes, "Why?" "What does that mean?" "Why did you say (or ask) that?" All comments, opinions, or statements made by students should be clarified to determine exactly what the student had in mind and the reasoning behind their contributions.

4) It is essential that the tutor avoids expressing an opinion concerning the correctness or quality of any student's comments or contributions.

5) It is also essential that the tutor avoids giving information to the students. Their information sources should be literature, faculty experts, automated information sources, models, specimens, field experiences, etc.

6) Discussions between students, comments and criticisms of each other's ideas or knowledge must always be encouraged.

7) All decisions should be a group process and have a group consensus. The tu ... must be certain that all students contribute to the group's activities.

8) The tut . should prevent discussions from being only between the tutor and students. He should do whatever is necessary to get the students to talk, discuss, and argue amongst themselves.

9) Challenges, particularly ones on the order of "Are you sure you're right?" or "Are you comfortable with that decision?" should be given to students when they are correct as often as when, in the mind of the tutor, they are incorrect in their opinions or statements.

10) The tutor should modulate the challenge of learning, to somewhere between boredom and being hopelessly over-challenged by learning tasks.

11) The tutor must monitor the quality of each student's educational progress and use metacognitive probes to establish or deny any concerns about adequacy of learning so that timely interventions and help, often from other students, can occur.

12) The tutor needs to be aware of potential interpersonal problems in the group and make the interventions necessary to maintain an effective group process in which all contribute. When the behavior of the group begins to adversly affect group progress and student learning, the group should take on their own problem as a dysfunctional group. It is an axiom that the students in the group do not have to like each other, but they must learn to work efficiently and assist each other as a group.

13) None of these tutorial activities should become the sole task of the tutor. The tutor must constantly work toward getting the group to take on responsibility for the group learning process, students asking each other and themselves the appropriate metacognitive questions as they proceed with their learning task. Eventually the tutor should become unnecessary as the group functions well on its own.

THE FIRST SESSION FOR
A NEW GROUP

Introductions

The first business for any new group, meeting for the first time, is to get to know each other and to establish ground rules. This important activity does not have to take up the entire session; learning can begin, but the time spent on this activity will save time in the long run in terms of the group's early efficiency and team work.

In a small working group, it is essential that each person has an opportunity to establish who they are and their own importance as an individual with unique and important things to offer by virtue of particular interests and background. We all like to feel important and have a need for strangers, with whom we are going to be working intimately and intensively, to know about us. These introductions should be brief, as no one wants to hear the life history of five strangers on the first day. However, a brief discussion by each will give all members of the group enough information to feel permitted to talk more with each other about common experiences, opinions and backgrounds. In fact, if each member does not have a chance to identify his own importance as an individual, he will often do this later through behaviors and comments that can interfere with the group process. Following such introductions, the group should feel more comfortable with each other and develop commonalities helpful for team work.

In addition, this initial discussion of backgrounds and interests can give the tutor an idea about the possible sources of information and expertise that might be available in the group. As a method for getting the members of a group to eventually take command of their own education, the tutor can defer to comments or opinions of students who may have special knowledge of information appropriate to the group's discussions. Also, with this awareness of each student's background, the tutor can guide students into unfamiliar areas of study during their learning, and avoid allowing them to continue learning in areas in which they are already familiar. The tutor should take notes during this introduction exercise as a start to an ongoing file on each student.

This initial period of introduction should remind the tutor and all the students in the group that the group is not a collection of students with blank slates in their minds, but a group of adults already knowledgeable and expert in many different areas. Actually, teachers are often amazed at the extent and richness of the backgrounds of students -- something that is never discovered, in more didactic, passive forms of education.

Each student is asked to introduce himself and briefly describe where he is from, where he went to school -- high school and university including post-graduate work, what kind of professional career does he anticipate pursuing and where, and any kinds of interesting jobs, experiences, travels, hobbies and interests. When each student finishes, the tutor should ask the other students in the group if they have any questions they would like to ask the student who just introduced himself in order to better understand his background. The tutor can model this behavior initially by asking such questions. In the same way, the tutor should also provide the students with his own background.

Establishing the Learning Climate

The educational climate in more traditional, didactic educational settings works against facilitatory tutorial teaching. In these settings, the student is expected to know the right answer. He learned a long time ago that it is best to stay silent if he does not know the answer, or is unsure of it, for he knows an admission of not knowing would be used as evidence of inadequate study or lack of intelligence. Unless a student has been in a more liberal or alternative school, this climate has usually been in existence throughout his educational career, kindergarten and beyond. It is a climate so taken for granted that students will automatically behave as if those same rules exist in the tutorial group. The other tacit assumption is that a student should never freely volunteer an alternative opinion about what the teacher or another student has said unless he is absolutely certain of what he is going to say. Both these unwritten rules work against learning in the small group.

The basic rule for effective learning in the small group format is that the student must be able to both recognize and freely admit that he does not know. Recognizing that you do not know is a great stimulus to learning. It is no sin not to know as no one can know all there is to know. Everyone is an expert in something, as the introductions should have revealed, but never in the same things. Some are ignorant in areas where others are well informed. Students are there to learn. An open and unembarrassed recognition and admission of not knowing or understanding by the student starts the chain of events that can lead to learning and full understanding. Further, it is appropriate for the student to describe what he thinks might be true. How else will he be challenged about the accuracy of his beliefs? Unspoken, and therefore unquestioned, incorrect beliefs may never be identified and will sit in the mind as a potential problem for further and more sophisticated understanding in related areas (McCloskey, Caramazza, Green, 1980).

The appropriate climate for a tutorial group is for the students to understand that there is nothing wrong with saying, "I don't know" to freely say what they think **might** be true -- even though they themselves may not be totally confident that they are right. Just stating this policy is not enough. It must be followed by behavior that establishes and reinforces this climate. It is important that the tutor freely admits when he does not know. He should never be seen as critical of any statements of ignorance or of any ideas offered by students, no matter how far off the mark or uninformed they might be.

Roles and Responsibilities

The tutor's responsibility is **guidance**. As a guide, he represents the faculty and is there to help the students achieve curricular goals and their own educational goals (see below). However, the students are expected to assume the same responsibility. They must realize that they are expected to take an increasingly larger portion of this responsibility until the tutor is no longer active. The educational responsibilities of the students in the small group tutorial method are far greater than in other teaching methods. They are expected to assume progressive responsibility for their group's progress and their own learning.

As mentioned in the previous section on climate, the students have a responsibility for being candid when they disagree with the ideas or opinions of others in the group, including the tutor.

Being open and candid about their own performance in the group (self-evaluation), as well as the performances of others, is also a responsibility for the students. Every time the group completes its work with a task or problem, each member has to evaluate his own performance and each other's (described later). The ability to do this in a frank, open, and constructive way is a must and so has to be practiced and developed. If a student is not carrying his share of the work or is not doing good work, the situation should be identified by others in the group. The quality of the learning process in a small group is dependent on the quality of the input of all members. The students must also learn to accept such criticism from their peers in a constructive way.

The students must also take responsibility for the maintenance of the group as a whole. If there are difficulties that develop in the function of the group -- personality clashes, an unproductive session, poor morale, whatever -- the students have the responsibility to identify such states of affairs.

The tutor might initiate the discussion of roles by asking the students what they think the tutor's role is in the group and what theirs should be? In the ensuing discussion, he can guide them into an understanding of his role through appropriate questions or challenges. However, with students totally new to the small group tutorial process, the tutor will have to make statements about his role and its rationale at appropriate points in the discussion. The same procedure can be used for a discussion of student roles and responsibilities.

MAJOR STAGES IN THE SMALL GROUP
TUTORIAL PROCESS

The foregoing steps are necessary for the initial meeting of the small tutorial group. The following steps represent stages in the group's process reasoning through a problem or task. This process may require two or more sessions. Characteristically the first session with a new problem or task has the students defining their objectives, reasoning their way through the problem or situation and identifying what they need to learn. This is followed by the students going off and carrying out self-directed learning to accomplish the identified learning needs. The second session follows when they return to apply what has been learned in self-directed study. If they find more needs to be learned during this application of their newly acquired knowledge, there may have to be more sessions held around that problem or task.

Learning Objectives

In any small working group it is important that every member of the group agrees on the group's objectives. What is it that the group wants to accomplish? What knowledge and skills do they wish to acquire in their work with the problem or task they have been assigned or have chosen? Without identified and agreed upon objectives, the individual students may be tacitly working towards different learning objectives based on their past behavior or individual interests; and the group may not accomplish what is expected in the curriculum or course.

Written curricular objectives designed by the faculty are the logical places to start. The students should be given a copy of such objectives and then asked how they would like to translate these into how the group should deal with the problems or tasks it will be working on. Students might wish to add to these objectives because of certain interests they have, or because of their realization that they have areas of weakness which need their extra concentration and attention.

Initially, this discussion of objectives may seem artificial and awkward. However, quite soon the group will drift into unimportant or unproductive, time-consuming areas, or side issues in its task. Or a divergence of opinions may develop among the members of the group over which issues or areas should be pursued. The objectives will serve as a guide to the appropriate direction and priorities. In time the value of good objectives as a guide will soon become apparent to the group and then discussions about objectives will become easier with subsequent problems. A discussion of objectives should occur before the group undertakes each new task, situation or problem.

Objectives help the tutor monitor and guide the group's learning process. When the students do wander off course, or get into disagreements about directions or priorities, the tutor can call their attention to it with comments such as: "There seems to be some disagreement as to where we should go next." "You all seem to be uncomfortable with where we are going." And if the students do not raise the question of the objectives they agreed upon, the tutor should. However, it is frequently valuable for the tutor, sensing a problem arising in the group, to let it play out awhile to see if any of the students identify the problem themselves and take the initiative to raise the issue of directions or priorities. They must take on responsibility for this monitoring after the tutor has modeled it for them a few times.

After the group gets underway and problems of directions and priorities arise, it may be obvious, on reflection of the agreed objectives, that they are not correct and need to be modified. Such midcourse corrections are certainly expected. Revision of objectives further helps the group to understand what its objectives really are, and to improve at expressing them. If the objectives are seen to be in need of modification, the modification must be agreed upon by the group.

Cognitive Processes Applied
to the Group's Task

In describing the tutor's role at the metacognitive level, the
reasoning or problem solving process required for the task,
situation or problem confronting the students in the group was
referred to a number of times. It was said that the tutor's
metacognitive challenges to the students should be those he
would use in his own mental reflections or deliberations about
the task, situation or problem. It was also said that one of the
important tasks for the tutor was to be certain that the
students considered each step of the appropriate reasoning or
problem solving process required for their task, applying what
they already knew during this process and deciding on what
they needed to learn to better understand and resolve the
problem or situation.

If the students are dealing with a real life problem or situation,
or a simulation of a real life problem or situation that is
"ill-structured," the usual procedural steps for problem solving
progress that have been identified as the hypothetico-deductive
process should be employed. The ill-structured problem is the
kind of problem we constantly face in life and certainly all
professionals face in their work. As described previously, when
the ill-structured problem presents itself, much of the
information that will be needed to evaluate and understand
what the problem is all about and to understand what has
caused the problem is not available at the outset. The patient
presenting with symptoms, the client with a legal problem, the
family in trouble, the electronic apparatus that will not work
correctly, the business that is not doing well, the poorly
performing employee, the bank with a suspected financial
irregularity, whatever, are all ill-structured. An inquiry has to
be undertaken to obtain the information needed to determine
the nature of the problem, what may be its cause, and then to
be able to effectively manage the problem. The problem solver
has to generate a number of possible causes for the problem
(hypotheses) to serve as a guide to his inquiry. We do this
almost automatically, but more creative explanations may have

to be thought of in difficult problems. Usually there is no magic formula or prescribed procedure for obtaining that information through inquiry; what is looked for on inquiry depends on what possibilities are being examined for the cause. Inquiry involves asking questions, observing, probing, examining, experimenting, to gain the needed information to build the picture of the entire problem (the **case** for the social worker, lawyer, physician, psychologist, detective). As this inquiry is undertaken and the important facts are assembled, the extent and character of the problem may change; it may not even resemble what it might have originally seemed to be. In this inquiry, there will be conflicting data, incomplete data, ambiguous data, and puzzlements or surprises can occur at any time. Often, the problem solver can never be truly certain he is right when he has concluded his analysis of the problem or case. Nevertheless, decisions have to be made so that the problem can be managed or resolved. The methods employed for resolution of the problem must be designed to address the assumed causes for the problem using whatever tools or techniques are appropriate. Most problems have to be followed to see if the methods for resolution are effective and whether more complications develop.

Well structured problems in which all the information needed to work the problem is present, the method to use for the solution of the problem is defined, and the problem solver gets a clear indication when the problem has been correctly solved and managed, occur only in textbooks.

This multiple hypothetico-deductive process is the appropriate cognitive response to the ill-structured problem and is the process used in studies of the cognitive processes of scientists and physicians. The writing of many scientists and the discussions I have had with people in other professions reinforce the wide spread use of this process. If a problem presents with insufficient data to determine what is going on (client or patient with the complaint, car that will not start, sales on an item that are not doing well, or a curious phenomenon that presents itself, etc. etc.), the problem solver has to imagine, from his own experience and knowledge, what the possibilities might be to explain the problem. He has to create, and usually always does create, a few ideas as to what might be going on (multiple hypotheses). These hypotheses serve him as a guide to the type and sequence of inquiries that need to be made (questions, probes, examinations, inspections, experiments). As information is obtained from inquiry it has to be analyzed for its relevance to the hypotheses entertained, or to decide whether new hypotheses need to be considered (analysis). He assembles the information gained through inquiry that is felt to be significant into a growing representation of the problem in his mind (problem synthesis). When blind alleys are encountered or inquiry reveals new aspects of the problem, the process becomes cyclic; new hypotheses are developed, new inquiry strategies are undertaken until at some point the problem solver feels as though he has narrowed down the possibilities and thinks that he has the most probable explanation for what is going on and what needs to be done about it.

This generic process has to be learned well through repeated practice so that it is efficient and effective, working well in tight, urgent, difficult or complex situations. It certainly represents the cognitive process that students in science fields, professional or preprofessional education (law, business, medicine, nursing, engineering) should use in the small tutorial group to deal with the problems, tasks and situations of the field of study. It seems ideal for students in other fields in which problem solving is a paramount skill (electronic trouble shooting, personnel management, auto repair, etc.). In conversations with teachers of mathematics, history, English and philosophy at college and high school levels, this process for teaching students in small groups seems attractive.

If the tutor for the small group uses his own reflections and deliberations as a guide for the students' process, the odds are that he will lead them through this process. However, a careful review by the tutor of what is known about the process and its various stages will enhance his ability to be an effective tutor at the metacognitive level. As mentioned previously, the tutor must be sure that the students go through each stage of the

process and consider their thinking as they work with the
problem; stages such as, generating hypotheses, developing an
inquiry strategy, analyzing new data in the light of entertained
hypotheses, synthesizing a growing problem description or
formulation from the significant new data obtained, and making
evaluative (diagnostic) and management (treatment) decisions.
This process, only briefly described here, is carefully defined for
tutors in medicine (Barrows and Tamblyn 1980, Barrows 1985)
and can provide guidance for tutors in other fields. (See Appendix I)

In guiding his students at the metacognitive level, the tutor
should not use jargon from studies in cognition such as "What
are your hypotheses at this point?" "Can we design an inquiry
strategy to establish the probable hypotheses?" (turning to a
student) "What is the problem synthesis to this point?"
although these are the appropriate metacognitive challenges.
The terms make a whole process that should be natural for
everyone, seem artificial and forced. If instead the tutor says,
to accomplish the same thing, "What kind of ideas do you have
at this point as to what might be going on with this problem?"
"So, what kinds of questions should we be asking to see which of
the ideas we have cooked up might be right?" (turning to a
student) "What do we know about this problem (case, patient)
at the present time, what are the important facts we should be
keeping in front of us as we problem solve?" Said in this way,
the metacognitive questions seem natural and stimulate
thinking in the students that seems reasonable and not
contrived.

In the traditional case method, as used in the Harvard Business
School, the process would be different. The students would
have read the needed information in the case and their
discussions would involve the building of hypotheses concerning
what the problems are in the case and their possible causes,
designing ways to resolve the problems, and defending these
ideas. In law, the process also involves the analysis of points of
law, prior cases and actions that are relevant to the case at
hand.

In art, architecture, art criticism, literature, etc., the process
may be different. Unfortunately there is not a body of studies
on how the expert in these fields thinks when practicing his art.
There are lots of conjectures, but they need to be looked at
carefully as many times the thinking of the expert is
unconscious and automatic. As we have learned in medicine,
you cannot assume what is going on in the expert's mind
through an analysis of his external behaviors. However,
lacking this knowledge of expert's thinking, the problem in the
small group tutorial teaching can be handled appropriately if
the tutor is a professional in the field. Such a tutor must
discipline himself to constantly reflect on what he would ask
himself at each stage in the task or situation facing the
students in his group, and use this as a basis for his
metacognitive questions and their sequence.

There are many other thinking formulas offered by many
authors in the area of problem solving that the tutor might
wish to employ, depending on the task, problems, or situations
used in the tutorial group. Baron (1981) modifies the problem
solving approach suggested by Dewey (see Baron), into the
following sequence: 1) problem recognition, 2) enumeration of
possibilities, 3) reasoning - the evaluation of possibilities
through a search for evidence, 4) revision of possibilities and, 5)
evaluation - should the process recycle or has the problem been
resolved?

Bransford and Stein (1984) offer the acronym "IDEAL" as an
approach to problem solving: 1) identify the problem, 2) define
and represent the problem, 3) explore possible strategies, 4) act
on strategies, and 5) look back and evaluate the effects of your
activities. There are many more.

With whatever sequence of reasoning activities the tutor uses,
the group should keep a record of their thinking on a
chalkboard or large pad; the ideas they had (hypotheses), the
inquiry strategies they used, the significant facts they have
acquired, and the conclusions they have come to. In this way
the group can critique their ideas and thinking after they have

gone off and learned the facts they need to understand and
resolve the problem (self-directed learning described below).

In this first session, before self-directed study, the students are
working with the task, problem or situations with their own
collective knowledge, the knowledge they bring to the problem.
In so doing, they realize what they actually already know and
what they will need to learn. This will make new learning more
meaningful and their study more productive.

Self-Directed Study

The need for all students to develop sound self-educational skills
as an effective, automatic behavior to continue their own
education for the rest of their lives was described at the
beginning. Self-directed learning is built into this small group
process as the tutor does not give the students information but
stimulates them to determine what they need to learn and how
to learn it on their own. The following phases of self-directed
learning should be incorporated throughout the problem solving
activities of the group. Steps 5 and 6 also represent a
continuation of the problem-solving process described above,
using new information they have acquired through self-directed
study.

1) Self-monitoring

As the students are working their way through a task or
problem, guided by the tutor's questions at the
metacognitive level, they are encouraged by the tutor to
indicate whenever they think their understanding,
knowledge base or reasoning skills are inadequate for the
task at hand and they would profit from further study or
review. Initially this is not a natural thing for many
students. The tutor has to model the process by sensing
hesitancy, perplexity, insecurity, or confusion in the
students' discussions and deliberations. At such points,
the tutor should ask whether the student thinks that there
is information he might like to look up, study or review, on

the topic under discussion. This should also be recorded on the same chalk board or large paper pad mentioned above to note down these areas of needed learning as the group's discussions are proceeding. The accumulated list can be reviewed later for self-directed learning assignments. Sometimes it helps for the tutor to ask the student to explain more fully an idea or comment he has expressed to see if the student then develops discomfort because of insufficient information or a lack of a true understanding about what he is trying to express. This insecurity can be often brought out by simply asking a student if he really knows what he is talking about, or how confident, on a scale of one to ten, he is that he is right in what he is saying? The student's admission of not being completely sure can again be followed by the question about whether a learning issue has been identified and needs to be written down.

The tutor will not have to do such obvious things after a short while as the process will soon sensitize students to an awareness of their need for more or better information. Soon students will begin asking each other whether a learning issue has been identified, or will identify their own need for a learning issue to be written down. Writing down these learning issues prevents the momentum of the group's work from being stopped as they can proceed on the basis of their present knowledge.

Occasionally, the group may get hung up in its progress because the knowledge they do not have becomes essential to their deliberations. If the missing knowledge represents a large and crucial area, the group may want to decide to stop at this point and go off and gain the knowledge through self-study before proceeding further. Often, the use of a handy, quick resource such as a dictionary or textbook may provide enough facts to go on, to be elaborated upon in later self-directed study. Such a decision has to be made by the group. On these occasions, it might use the tutor as such a resource if he is an expert in the area of knowledge needed. This role change should not become a habit and should be used to provide only an isolated bit of knowledge to enable the problem solving process to continue. The tutor should not elaborate beyond the facts asked for, or give a discussion, but just answer the question.

2) Formalizing what needs to be learned

When the students have worked as far as possible on the problem, task or situation with their present, collective knowledge and ability, and have committed themselves to a decision about the nature of the problem or situation, its cause and possibly its resolution, the tutor then guides them through a review of the learning issues that were written down during their discussions. The tutor might ask if there are ways that the list might be better organized or categorized? The group should consider the learning objectives it created at the outset to see if these learning issues might be better phrased or tuned to accomplish the agreed-upon objectives. Once this has been done, the group should be asked whether it wants to divide up the learning issues among its members or whether each wants to look up all of them. This decision is often determined by the size of the learning list. Even if the students divide the issues among themselves, they can be encouraged to consider looking into the other topics as well to see if what they learn matches with what others learn. The tutor can often prime this process by identifying students in the group who raised particular learning issues that seemed important to them at the time they were raised in the ongoing group discussion.

If the students in the group come from diverse backgrounds, it is important for the tutor to suggest that the students each take learning issues in areas totally unfamiliar to them for their own individualized self-directed learning. For example, in the small group process in medical school, the biology major should be encouraged to take on the psychological or epidemiological learning issues and the student with a psychology major to take on the biological issues. Too frequently students will pick study issues in areas in which they are already familiar.

3) Selecting learning resources

The effective and efficient acquisition of knowledge and skills requires an awareness of the wide range of resources available for learning, and their particular advantages and disadvantages in terms of availability, accessibility, time, effort, cost as opposed to their value. The dimension of value concerns contemporaneousness and accuracy or reliability. The range of resources includes human resources (faculty, consultants, practitioners, experts), printed resources (books, journals, monographs, reviews, technical reports, abstracts), automated or computerized information resources, specimens, models, atlases, and field experiences (clinics, research laboratories, digs, construction, etc.) The tutor asks each student to identify the particular resources each plans to use to satisfy their chosen learning issues and the rationale for the selection. The tutor must encourage the students to use resources that are not those they would routinely use such as textbooks and reference books. They should be encouraged to use faculty members and more contemporaneous printed or automated resources for their learning. During their study, all students should be encouraged to do the following:

a) Make a list of particularly good references to distribute to the other students in the group for their own review and personal filing systems;

b) Make duplicates of any particularly excellent articles, or lists, diagrams or summaries they might have made for themselves, for the others in the group;

c) Bring in any useful illustrations, models, specimens, or even persons that they feel would contribute to the group's understanding of the learning issues involved.

The group should list the learning issue assignments of each member as this will be useful when the problem is tackled again to indicate at which point each student has a contribution to make (see No. 6, "The application of new learning").

4) Negotiating the time for self-directed learning

The tutor should get the students to decide on the length of time that will be needed to accomplish their self-directed learning tasks. The length of time is usually determined by the number of learning issues involved and the complexity and availability of the resources chosen. This, of course, is not possible in a curriculum that schedules the time of tutorials and the time available for self-directed learning. As self-directed learning becomes more effective and efficient, the time required is reduced.

5) Resource critique

(This step and step 6 represent a return to the cognitive, problem-solving activity that was occurring in the first session before self-directed study). When the students return after their self-directed study to apply what they have learned to the problem or task at hand, the tutor first asks them to each describe what resources they actually did use during their self-directed study and to critique them. They will have frequently found deficiencies in the resources they thought they would use (too simple or superficial, too complex or diffuse, did not have the information expected, unavailable, etc.) and may have resorted to others. Initially students are frustrated by their inability to find the resource they needed, or to know how to use it (particularly library and computerized automated information resources). Finding the right resource is difficult and it takes practice.

In this critique, the tutor should make sure that the students do not describe **what** they learned from the resource, just critique it as a resource. When the students

describe the difficulties they had, the tutor can use
metacognitive questions to amplify the critique of the
resources. He should ask those questions he would have
asked himself about the resource such as, "What was the
date of publication of that book?" "Who are the authors,
are they authorities in the field?" "How did you go about
finding that information, what were your search words?"
"How do you know that information is reliable?" The other
students should be asked to comment on the frustrations
and problems each student had with resources. Other
students might have suggestions for resources they
thought were better, or better ways to get at resources,
even better ways to get by a faculty member's secretary for
a consultaton. When the student has finished his critique
of the resources he used, he should be asked to describe
what he would have done differently if he were to start to
research the same learning issues over again.

As experience with the critique of learning resources
progresses, the tutor should begin to question the
student's ability to assess the reliability of the information
he obtains from research articles. Students should learn
to assess research design, data analysis, and the
conclusions drawn in a research article. This in itself may
lead to the development of learning issues and further
self-study in references about research design, data
analysis, etc.

6) The application of new learning

It should be assumed by the tutor that after the students
have returned from their period of self-directed learning,
they must know everything that they thought they needed
to know to understand and resolve the problem that they
were working on. The tutor should now consider them
"experts" in solving the problem or situation at hand.

The students are often quite excited about what they have
learned and the insights and knowledge their new
learning has given them about the problem at hand.

However, the tutor should make sure that the group's study does not degenerate into a "show and tell" at this point. The power of their new learning will be lost if they just sit there and, in essence, lecture to each other about what they have learned in their study. The tutor must now ask the students to start over with the problem or situation from the very beginning and describe what they now realize they should have thought and done with the problem (hypotheses, inquiry strategy, synthesis, decisions, etc.), based on their new learning. As they do this, they should compare their new thinking with what they had thought and done previously. The tutor makes certain that they again consider each step in the same sequence of cognitive events as before. The tutor, by his questions and comments can highlight this comparison so that the students realize how they should have reasoned and now have a chance to apply their new learning. Information from **each student's self-directed learning is then brought into the picture at the point the issue was raised in the prior discussions** so the new knowledge can be applied to the problem and integrated into what is already known. This is a very educationally powerful stage in the group process as students critique prior knowledge and reasoning and apply new knowledge as they reason, linking reasoning skills and knowledge into their respective long-term memory banks.

The tutor's role is the same as previously; he challenges them with the metacognitive questions appropriate in this application of new knowledge, and critique of past thinking. He can ask for fuller explanations, comments from others, and particularly for statements that students might now be able to make that would integrate and solidify what has been learned.

It is quite possible that in this application of new knowledge to the problem, new learning issues are raised as further unanswered questions arise, or if the new knowledge gained did not answer all of the questions raised previously. The group may have to go off for more self-directed learning and start the cycle again.

7) Debriefing (the conscious integration of what has been learned).

Once the group has finished its work with a problem, situation or task, it must reflect on what it has learned. Much of what has been learned will undoubtedly be recalled by the students whenever they face future problem or situation contexts similar to the one the group was working with. This is characteristically a non-verbal recall; the student may just do the right thing with a future problem without exactly knowing why (Schon's "knowing in action"). If this debriefing step is not undertaken in the small group process, what has been learned may not be consciously recalled by students for transfer to other problem contexts or in future written or verbal tests. It is also important for the students in the group to be able to understand how the new knowledge they have acquired fits into their general knowledge of the disciplines that were involved in self-directed study. In medicine, for example, how has work with a patient problem extended their knowledge of anatomy, physiology, clinical diagnosis, etc?

The tutor initiates this final step by asking "What have we learned with this problem, what new facts or concepts?" and later, "How has our work with this problem extended our knowledge of the anatomy of the nervous system?" (for example). This will seem difficult for students initially, and, as with everything else, the tutor will have to model the process by suggesting things, relevant to the objectives of the course, that he knows they have learned. It helps to ask the students to diagram relationships, develop lists or talk about other applications of the knowledge obtained. The intent is to get them to recognize, verbalize, review and integrate what has been learned.

8) Evaluation

The ability to evaluate self and others with accuracy and in a positive and constructive way is a skill that can also be learned, through practice, in the small group tutorial process. These are lifetime skills important for the student. If the student is to assume responsibility for his own learning, he has to be able to assess his ability to work with a problem or task accurately. Once students acquire good self-assessment skills, they can provide their own evaluation at the end of their course of study.

At the end of each unit, completion of a problem or task, the tutorial group should undergo a formal evaluation session. Each student should be asked to describe how he thought he did with that unit in terms of the following:

a) Reasoning through the problem (problem solving)

b) Self-directed learning (identifying learning issues, finding appropriate resources, bringing new information to the group for work on the problem)

c) Support of the group process.

When each student has finished his critique of his own performance, the tutor should invite other students to comment on that evaluation and add their own opinions about the student's performance. Initially, students are very polite to each other and usually disagree with another student's evaluation of his own performance only if they feel he was too critical of himself and can therefore be positive in their feedback by reassuring the student that he was not as bad as he said he was. Again, they need to see modelling by the tutor for more frank and constructive opinions. If a student's performance was weak or unsatisfactory and neither the student himself or the other students comment on it, the tutor should with comments such as, "Actually I thought you were unable to see beyond that one idea

you had for the problem, and it limited your ability to
see its real implications." "Those resources you went to
seemed to be rather superficial and you didn't bring the
kind of information we needed to really understand."
"You seemed to want to take over the group's thinking
and tell everyone what should be asked and how it
should be put together." Once the students have the
freedom to express their opinions about each other,
particularly after the group process gets underway and
the students become dependent on the quality of each
other's work and study for their own learning, they will
become very accurate and critical. This peer pressure
for good performance is very effective and not found in
other educational methods. In time, each student
becomes both more aware and accurate about his own
performance.

SHOULD THE TUTOR BE AN EXPERT?

W ith a class of 100 students, there will need to be 16 to 20 tutors as the small group cannot function well beyond eight members. If there are more some students will become lost to the tutor as it is hard to have active interactions with all students (see the next section). It may be difficult for a school to have a sufficient staff of teachers to provide this many tutors that are experts in the discipline or field being taught in the small group facilitatory method. Many teachers are uncomfortable about being a tutor in an area with which they are unfamiliar, even though they realize that the students will actually be learning facts from learning resources such as appropriate discipline experts on the faculty and books, and **not** from them. They are concerned that not being experts in the subject under study they will be unable either to guide the students into the most important areas of learning or to adjudge whether the facts acquired and ideas expressed are correct or not.

There is no question that the ideal circumstance is for the tutor to be expert both as a tutor and in the discipline being studied by the students. However, if this is not possible, the next best tutor is the teacher who is good at being a tutor, as described here, though not an expert in the discipline being studied. There are some excellent tutors who are quite comfortable being a tutor in an area in which they have sparse personal knowledge, as they feel secure in their facilitatory skills. Their metacognitive challenges are truly representative of their own thinking as they are also working through an unfamiliar problem along with the group. They can truly say to their students that they cannot be expected to teach any facts since they know little about the field of study. Students are frequently upset by tutors who they know are experts but refuse to give them any facts or tell them if they are on the right track.

As the skill of the tutor is the backbone of the small group learning process, it is **not acceptable** to have a teacher who is an **expert** in the area of study, but a **weak** tutor.

Given an inexpert tutor, there are some things that can be done to help him feel comfortable in his inexpert role:

1) Have well stated curricular objectives so that both he and his students know what is to be accomplished.

2) Provide him with a set of learning issues that the faculty feel should be identified by students with every problem, task or situation used in the group.

3) Orient the tutor about each problem, task and situation to be used. Identify their importance in the curriculum, why they were chosen, what the student should learn from them, and any particularly important points about traps or difficult issues that could arise.

4) Provide the tutor with an expert with whom he can consult at any time and who might on occasion come to a tutorial group session to listen to the group's deliberations and give feedback about its understanding and progress.

A related issue, mentioned above, but which probably needs to be discussed is the concern of the nonexpert tutor that his students may be saying incorrect things and learning incorrect things and neither he nor they would ever know. The steps described above should help to alleviate this concern. Nevertheless, this is not too likely a problem if the tutor keeps all the students involved and always provokes students to challenge each other. Students are well known for their well developed "crap detectors," which are usually more sensitive than the teacher's. In a group of five to seven students, there will always be one or more who will identify errors in other students' comments and bring evidence to prove it. Also, when students go off on their self-directed learning, seeking information in references and from faculty, they **will** come back with the correct ideas. It is important to ask students to back up any terms they use, elaborate more fully on ideas expressed, and prove their statements are correct.

LARGE GROUP TUTORING

These tutorial skills can be used with large groups, up to about a hundred students. Such an approach may be attractive to schools or institutions where sufficient numbers of well prepared tutors to guide smaller groups are not available. This offers many of the same advantages that small group work offers over lectures and other forms of passive learning as it allows the students to benefit from many of the advantages of facilitatory learning. (Barrows et al., 1986) They will be challenged to develop and practice reasoning skills, to develop skills in self-directed learning, and to actively apply what has been learned. Similar to the case method, it provides active learning that is motivating for students. There are, of course, obvious drawbacks to this use of tutorial skills when compared to small group work:

1) The excitement and pleasure of working on a close, personal basis with a small group of students is lost to both the students and the tutor;

2) Not all students would get an opportunity to express their opinions, adding their contributions, and their individual ideas and concerns into the ongoing deliberations of the group;

3) The tutor is unable to monitor each student's educational growth and to detect problems early in the student's learning process thus making it impossible for the tutor to provide early educational assistance to the student -- when it is most effective.

The first key to the employment of these tutorial skills to a large group is for the tutor to be surrounded by the students who then face each other, which is more conducive to a free-flowing discussion between them. The usual classroom arrangement has the students all facing forward towards the teacher and exchanges between students are extremely difficult as they cannot see each other unless they turn their necks back and forth, and they usually cannot hear each other well. Therefore, a "U" shaped arrangement of chairs is best. The second key is to have assigned seating for the students and for the tutor to have a seating chart to allow him to identify each student by name.

If the students are working from a case, they each should have a copy of the case to work with and preferably have had a chance to study the case before coming to the session with the tutor. The tutor's procedure differs from the case method only in that he interacts with the group at the metacognitive level in his questions and challenges and does not give information or indicate when discussion or comments from students are correct or incorrect. He can begin with "What is going on in this problem?" or "Who wants to start off here?"

As the session proceeds, the tutor will also have to carry out the same focused tasks as discussed previously, making sure all students eventually contribute, challenging them to explain more fully or define what they are talking about, challenging students who are correct in their comments as often as those who are not, etc. The ability to know where all students are in their learning is, as mentioned, far less possible. Nevertheless, after a few sessions, the tutor can get to know who is on target, who is in potential difficulty and who needs to be watched. The seating chart is invaluable as the tutor can select the student from whom he wants a response, ignoring the one who is always on target and challenging the one that seems mystified or baffled (or does not seem to be concentrating on the discussions). This not only provides the tutor with diagnostic feedback about the students who are doing well and those who may not be doing well, but it also keeps all the students involved, as they never know when they are going to be selected for an opinion. In fact, they will soon realize at an unconscious level that if they seem distracted or not paying attention, they will get called upon to contribute. This is so different from the small tutorial group in which the tutor can expect all students to get their opinions into the discussion or when he can say, "What do you all think of this?" and get opinions from all students. The tutor should acknowledge the students who are eager to comment in response to something another student has said, and afterwards, should look at the student who made the original comment to see if a rebuttal or further comment can be encouraged. Using this kind of approach and by saying, "Does anyone want to comment on that?" the students in the class will soon start interacting with each other, and the tutor can step out to the opening in the "U" to allow the discussion to go on. The tutor can then interject only as necessary to keep the discussions on track and the process moving. As in the small group process, the tutor should soon be able to withdraw from the class, off to the side as the learning process continues. This is where the "U" shaped arrangement of students pays off.

To be sure that all students understand what is going on and are all at similar points in learning, the tutor should occasionally ask the students to take out a piece of paper, put their name on it, and give their answer, opinion, ideas, on the topic under discussion at that moment. To make sure that all students take on a particular learning issue, the tutor can ask all students to answer questions about that issue when they come to the next session. This can also be done for items brought out at the last session. These snap written quizzes can help the tutor see if there is a general problem in understanding or whether certain students are having difficulties.

If the problem-based learning process is to be used, the problem must be presented to the large group as it occurred in real life, i.e., as an ill-structured problem, and then multiple hypotheses generated, an inquiry process undertaken to build the case, new information analyzed and the significant information obtained added to the growing synthesis of the problem (Barrows and Feltovich 1987). (See Appendix I) This can be done in a number of ways. The tutor can present the patient problem orally. He can then provide the information obtained from questions asked of the patient by the group, physical examination items performed, and, later, the laboratory tests requested by the class. As in the small group process, the tutor will be shaping and challenging this performance with the appropriate metacognitive questions that involve these phases and probe the depths of the students' understanding. The tutor can record the collected ideas of the class on a chalk board along with the learning issues raised in the interactive process. If available, a computerized version of the problem can be used with monitors around the class. With printed problems, each student can be given a copy of the problem.

Similar approaches can be used by tutors in other disciplines using simulations of the real life tasks the students will face as the stimulus for reasoning and learning.

Self-directed learning is facilitated by dividing the large class into smaller working groups of six to eight students with an identified recorder for each group. The learning issues can then be taken by each group for its members to work on together, coming back with a summary report with references etc. and then, as in the small group process, add their contribution to the review of the task or problem. The summary reports can be duplicated for the reference files of all students.

In Summary

The major points for the tutorial process are these. The tutor is responsible for the **process of learning**. He facilitates student learning through guidance at the **metacognitive level**. In this process he does not overtly give the students information or indications that he thinks they are right or wrong in their thinking. It is the tutor's expertise **in this process,** not in the content areas in which the students are studying, that is important. The students are expected to acquire the knowledge they need from content experts on the faculty who serve as consultants, as well as books, journals, and automated information sources, just as they will have to when they are out working in the real world. The tutor guides the students through repeated practices in reasoning and self-directed study, improved through their increasing skills in self-assessment. Although the tutor may be more directive initially and closely models the reasoning processes and information seeking processes he hopes the students will acquire, he eventually withdraws from the group as they learn to take on responsibility for their own learning. The whole process is comprised of: confronting a new problem, situation or task; problem solving by reasoning through the problem to determine its cause, and deciding on appropriate management; sensing educational needs to better handle the problem, task or situation; finding and using appropriate learning resources to fill those needs; applying that new information to that task or problem, as well as others like them. This is the process you want the student to continue to exercise and perfect throughout his life and career. The small group tutorial process should provide the student with the metacognitive skills he will need to do this - as he has learned to learn in contexts and practices relevant to his future.

APPENDIX I

THE PB/SDL TUTORIAL PROCESS
A Sequence of Tutorial Steps Essential to Achieving Full benefit From Problem-based, Self-directed Learning

This is designed as a supplement to The Tutorial Process as this book was designed to facilitate tutorial processes that might be applied in many different fields or professions. This supplement outlines the sequence of steps used in problem-based, self-directed learning in medicine that has the development of the clinical reasoning process as an educational goal (Barrows 1986) as it incorporates the multiple-hypothetico deductive process used by physicians to resolve the type of problems that are presented by patients. (Barrows and Pickell 1991) Many of the stages described here are covered in the book in more detail.

> ### AT THE FIRST MEETING OF A NEW TUTORIAL GROUP

Introductions
The students each describe their background, prior education, reasons for entering medical school, anticipated career in medicine, as well as experiences/ hobbies/ employment that could be of interest to the group. This allows each student to identify himself/ herself as a person, students to identify common interests, and for the group to realize potential sources of information and expertise within the group. The tutor introduces himself/herself in a similar manner.

Climate
The tutor sets a working climate of openness, and encourages students to say what ever is in their minds. The tutor also requests that whenever any student has information or an opinion that differs from that being expressed in the group the

student should speak up. An assumption will be made that if no one else speaks up when someone is presenting information or ideas, then everyone agrees with what is being said.

THE FIRST SESSION WITH A NEW PROBLEM

Objectives

The group should review the course objectives and their own interests to determine what is the focus for learning. As a patient problem could be the stimulus for a years curriculum, the group needs to decide what they wish to learn from their work with this problem. In the preclinical years of medical school, the objectives are usually to determine the basic science mechanisms responsible for the patient's problem; what anatomical structures, physiological systems, biochemical or behavioral mechanisms are involved. As the group proceeds with new problems they may wish to emphasize particular objectives based on their experience with previous problems. Objectives setting often seems difficult initially and the process can be helped by the tutor discussing the objectives for the curricular unit the group is in and their rationale.

Approach to the Problem Simulation

The simulations commonly used in tutorial groups are PBLMs (Distlehorst and Barrows 1982) and standardized (simulated) patients (Barrows 1987), depending on the objectives of the group. The PBLM is a convenient, portable patient simulation format that presents the cognitive challenges of a patient problem as it allows for free inquiry into the patient's problem through history, physical examination and laboratory investigations. In addition, the standardized patient allows the students to practice and learn history, physical examination, interpersonal, and professional skills. Each simulation sacrifices some important aspect of clinical reality and has some problems in use. All this is discussed by the tutor (for example, with the PBLM, the students have to decide on each question, item of physical examination, and laboratory test to be used and the justification for each action in the light of hypotheses considered before taking that action, whereas in the real clinical situation they can ask numerous questions in rapid sequence).

The tutor also asks the student nearest the blackboard to divide it into three main sections and one smaller section: The main ones are for: ideas generated about the possible causes for the patient problem (hypotheses); the significant facts generated through hypothesis guided inquiry (facts); and the learning issues that appear during the groups work with the problem (learning issues). The fourth, smaller area notes future action that the group may want to take later with the problem, such as ordering certain laboratory tests or diagnostic studies.

The next six steps represent stages in the clinical reasoning process (Barrows and Pickell 1991) and the tutor is careful to ensure that the group is involved with each of these, as this is a logical and natural process for clinical problem solving and the one used by experienced clinicians. The students are often unaware of the tutor's influence in guiding them through these stages.

The tutor is also alert to areas where students seem confused or unsure of themselves and helps them to recognize that there is a learning issue that needs to be put on the board--especially if it is an area relevant to the learning the problem is expected to generate.

1) Patient and Situation
The presenting picture of the patient and the health care situation is considered, including any accompanying photographs of the patient or patient records, to frame the nature of the problem confronted from the cues available at the outset.

2) Hypothesis generation
Based on the presenting picture and the way the problem has been framed the group attempts to generate as many ideas about the possible causes or explanations (diagnoses) they can think of on the basis of their own past experiences and knowledge. Freedom to be creative in this process is encouraged. These are recorded on the black board section named "ideas" (hypotheses).

3) Inquiry
Using the list of ideas (hypotheses) that were generated the group determines the questions that should be asked of the patient in an attempt to verify or deny those ideas. As the process continues they will determine the items of physical examination that should be performed to continue to refine their

ideas. Finally the group may determine the laboratory tests that would help further confirm or deny the ideas (hypotheses) remaining. If the acquisition of basic science knowledge is an objective of the group, this inquiry should be aimed at elucidating the basic mechanisms responsible for the patient's problem down to the organ, tissue or molecular level.

4) Data analysis
As the inquiry is undertaken, each item of new information gained about the patient and the patient's problem is analyzed by the group against the ideas (hypotheses) that were generated for its ability to verify or deny any of them; or possibly cause new ones to be generated. As data accumulates about the patient the hypotheses are frequently reviewed to see if they can be strengthened, denied, or new ones should be generated.

5) Problem synthesis
As the inquiry and analysis proceeds all new information that is felt to be significant, in the light of the hypotheses being considered, is recorded under "facts" on the black board. Occasionally a student in the group is asked to summarize the important data obtained about the patient, without referring to the blackboard, to make certain that the entire group is working on the same mental representation of the problem. This summarization develops students' ability to present patient data in an organized fashion. After such a summary is given, and agreed upon by the group, it a good time to review the ideas (hypotheses) in detail to see if in the light of this synthesis they need to be reorganized in different hierarchies, some eliminated, or new ones added. The appropriate inquiry path may be reconsidered. This is a good mechanism for getting the groups discussion back on track when it becomes diffuse and rambling.

6) Commitment as to the cause for the problem
The above processes (hypothesis generation-inquiry, analysis-synthesis) continues until the group has gone as far as they can go on their present accumulated knowledge in analyzing the problem and possibly suggesting way to treat and manage it. At this point each member of the group is asked to make a commitment as to what they each think might be responsible for the problem (and how to treat it), even though they do not have as much information as they would like at this point (this

provides a strong motivation for self- directed learning to verify the correctness of their public commitment).The opinion of each is recorded.

7) Identifying the learning issues to be studied
Throughout this entire problem-solving process, the students have been encouraged to identify things that they need to learn to better analyze the problem and areas that they are not sure of or would like to review. As these were identified during their work with the problem, they were listed on the black board under "learning issues." After they have made their commitment as to the causes and possibly the treatment for the problem (above) the group reviews these learning issues and their relevance to the objectives initially agreed upon. They then each choose individual learning issues they will take a responsibility for researching (even though the group as a whole may review all of them to some extent). Students are encouraged by the tutor to take on learning issues in areas that they are unfamiliar with, or have little background in, and to avoid areas in which they do possess experience and knowledge.

8) Identifying the learning resources to be used
Before embarking upon self-directed learning each student is asked to describe the learning resources they plan to use. The tutor encourages them to use primary sources of information and to use experts in the faculty in consultation (resource faculty). Each student is asked to bring references they found useful, notes they may have made, and to copy diagrams or illustrations that could be helpful resources for the group.

9) Self-directed learning
The time that is needed for the learning issues and resources identified is negotiated as is the time and place the group will meet to continue the process.

AFTER SELF-DIRECTED LEARNING

---

1) Resource critique
Each student is asked to describe the learning resources they actually ended up using in their self-study, not what they learned, but what they used to get the needed information. They are asked to critique these resources in terms of the accuracy

and value of the information found. Whenever a problem with resources is uncovered he group is asked to comment on how a better resource might have been found. The tutor uses this discussion to promote concerns about accuracy of information.

2) Reassessment of the problem: application of new knowledge to the problem and the critique of prior thinking and knowledge. Now that the students have completed their self-directed study and learned everything they felt they needed to know about the problem encountered, they are considered experts and should start with the problem over again to critique their prior thinking and knowledge used in the first session. They are asked to considered what, in the light of their new learning, their hypotheses should have been, what questions should have been asked, and how the problem should have been analyzed and understood. At the appropriate times in this process the information learned during self-study is discussed and applied to the problem.

3) Summary and integration of what has been learned
Once the students feel they have finished in their work with the problem and their learning related to the problem, they are asked to described what they have learned in words, discussions, diagrams, and definitions. They compare this problem with similar problems in the past and how their learning with this problem should prepare them for similar problems in the future. These discussions can lead to the development of major principles or concepts in the particular curriculum domain they are in.

4) Evaluation
Each student is asked to evaluate his/her own performance in three areas: problem-solving; self-directed learning; and support of the group with its tasks. After each student has done this, the rest of the group is asked to comment on that self-evaluation, adding constructive comments from their own perception of the student's performance. The tutor is included in this process of self-evaluation with critique from the group. The final evaluation of each student in the course and the evaluation of the tutor should be derived from this activity. Self- evaluation is an essential component of effective self-directed education.

APPENDIX II

A Series of Hypothetical Tutor-student Interactions

In the series of hypothetical tutor-student interactions set out below, all, except the first, are facilitatory. Each subsequent interaction is more facilitatory and offers less direct guidance than the preceding.

The students and tutor are in a problem-based learning session using a printed patient problem simulation that allows for free inquiry. The responses of the students in this hypothetical set of scenarios are based on my use of this problem with many different students in many different medical schools. It is hypothetical in that I have not used all of the tutorial approaches outlined with this particular problem - although I have used a number of them. The advantages of each are discussed.

Each interaction is lettered sequentially, T = tutor, S = student.

The students have just learned that the patient has difficulty swallowing. Whenever she attempts to do so she gags and some of the fluid she attempts to swallow comes out her nose.

██

T: This symptom is caused by a paralysis of the pharyngeal muscles. You can tell because not only is she not able to swallow, but also fluid comes out of her nose. With paralysis of the pharyngeal muscles, you cannot initiate swallowing and form water or food into a bolus to enter the esophagus. Also, you cannot keep the soft palate firmly against the posterior pharyngeal wall. That permits fluid to rush up into the hypopharynx and out the nose. Therefore, the combination of difficult swallowing **and** fluid through the nose always tells you that you are dealing with pharyngeal paralysis.

(Here the tutor does not know anything about the student's prior knowledge in this matter or whether he understood all or any part of what was said. The length of time the student will remember this should be a concern.)

(B)

T: What does this mean?

S: I don't know.

T: This symptom is caused by a...............etc.etc. (as above)

(At least the tutor knows that the student does not recognize the significance of the symptom and information is needed. How deep the student's ignorance may go is not known, nor whether the student understands what was said)

(C)

T: What does this mean?

S: I don't know.

T: Please guess, what do you think?

S: There is an obstruction in her throat.

T: No, this symptom is caused by a . . . . etc. (as above)

(Although not much further ahead, at least the student has committed himself and also realizes he does not know what the symptom means. His forced commitment, by being asked to guess, will capture his curiosity as to whether he was right or wrong and increase his attention to the tutor's remarks.

The realization that he was wrong will probably make the student better remember facts that are subsequently offered by the tutor).

(D)

T: What does this mean?

S: I don't know.

T: Please guess, what do you think?

S: There is an obstruction in her throat.

T: That wouldn't cause fluids to come out her nose, try again.

(The student made a commitment and will pay attention, as above. He not only realizes that he was probably wrong, he also learns he will have to give reasons for any comments he makes. After his guess on the cause of the symptom was obviously shown to be wrong by virtue of the tutor's response, he now learns that his reasons for his decision were also wrong. He is still left guessing. He realizes that nasal regurgitation does not go with obstruction in the throat. He is stimulated to begin to look at features that could identify the cause of the symptom. It is apparent to this student that this is not going to be the usual listen-to-the-teacher situation, and he is going to have to think. Attention and thinking must be going into gear).

(E)

T: What does this mean?

S: I don't know.

T: Please guess, what do you think?

S: There is an obstruction in her throat.

T: Why do you think so?

S: She can't swallow.

T: What else did you notice?

S: Fluids come out of her nose when she tries to swallow.

T: Does this happen with throat obstruction?

S: I'm not sure.

T: Well, it doesn't. What do you think now?

(The tutor realizes now that the student did not just fail to notice the complaint of nasal regurgitation, he did notice it but does not know what nasal regurgitation signifies. The student knows that he was wrong, unlike the true tutorial situation, however, the tutor has again given information).

(F)

T: What does this mean?

S: I don't know.

T: Please guess, what do you think?

S: There is an obstruction in her throat.

T: Why do you think so?

S: When she tries to swallow, nothing can go down her esophagus, so it must be obstructed.

T: There are a lot of reasons for not being able to swallow. What else makes you think it is an obstruction?

(Much of the foregoing applies about the attention getting effects of making a commitment. The student's attention is heightened as he still does not know whether he is right or wrong. Here the tutor learns something about the student's reasoning and knowledge. The student is now forced not only to display his opinion but is also forced to give reasons for it. The tutor makes it apparent that there are other causes for the complaint and that the student's reason does not serve to distinguish one from the other - an insufficient cause for an inference).

(G)

T: What does this mean?

S: I don't know.

T: Please guess, what do you think?

S: There is an obstruction in her throat.

T: Why do you think so?

S: When she tries to swallow, nothing can go down her esophagus, so it must be obstructed.

T: Maybe she isn't trying to swallow, she takes in food, holds it in her mouth, and then gags and spits it out. Maybe food nauseates her?

(This has all the elements as described above. However, at the end the tutor did not tell him that his reason for his inference was inadequate, he demonstrated it by offering a counterexample, an example based on the student's observation that nothing would go down her throat. If continued, this dialog should force the student to bring out tacit knowledge about the mechanisms of swallowing he may know but is not verbalizing. Hopefully! It makes it clear to the student that any reason chosen should distinguish an obstruction in the throat from everything else that could be responsible for her complaint).

(H)

T: What does this mean?

S: I don't know.

T: Please guess, what do you think?

S: There is an obstruction in her throat.

T: Why do you think so?

S: When she tries to swallow, nothing can go down her esophagus, so it must be obstructed.

T: What else do you notice?

S: She regurgitates fluids through her nose when she tries to swallow.

T: Does that occur with obstruction in the throat?

S: I'm not sure.

T: What else do you notice?

(Tension mounts in the student, unlike previous settings, the tutor is giving no hints as to his own thinking and continues to probe. The tutor has undoubtedly made the student unsure about his knowledge in the area of whatever is going on. It is clear to the student that observations that are significant are being asked for and that his knowledge is on the line. When this episode is over, it would be the rare student who would not go and find out what is going on).

(I)

T: What does this mean?

S: I don't know.

T: Please guess, what do you think?

S: There is an obstruction in her throat.

T: Why do you think so?

S: When she tries to swallow, nothing can go down her esophagus, so it must be obstructed.

T: What else do you notice?

S: She regurgitates fluids through her nose when she tries to swallow.

T: Does that occur with obstruction in the throat?

S: I'm not sure.

T: What do you know for sure about the anatomy and physiology of swallowing.'

S: I think that it would be highly unlikely for a woman of her young age to have anything wrong with swallowing unless something like a tumor or something was blocking the back of her throat, or maybe upper esophagus. If the opening is too narrow you can't swallow.

T: Do you think it might be worth while to look up the mechanics of swallowing, and what might be responsible for the inability to do so in this young lady?

S: I suppose it would.

T: Could it be anything else, think of all the possibilities?

S: There could be a lot I suppose.

T: What other causes can you think of that might look pretty much like this?

S: I can't think of too many others, maybe her throat muscles are paralyzed for some reason and she can't swallow.

T: What do you know about the control of the throat muscles?

S: (describes what he knows)

T: So how are you going to decide what this is - what more do you need to know?

(We have arrived at the truly facilitatory tutor. The student has been given a strong stimulus to study built upon an awareness of the extent of his ignorance. The tutor has given no indication of whether he thinks the student is right or wrong. Even when the student made the right diagnosis, he was not given the satisfaction of being right. If he learned that his second guess was right, the impetus to dig out knowledge in this area would be diminished).

APPENDIX III

Outlines for the Three Architectural Structures of the Tutorial Process

I.The **structure** of the teaching/learning sequences in problem-based learning

    A)The first time the group meets:

        1)Introductions and background of each member.

        2)Establishing the climate and ground rules.

    B)The first session with a new problem.

        1)Establish **learning objectives**.

        2)**Evaluate and manage the problem**, as far as possible, with the present knowledge and skills possessed by the group. The problem is taken on as an unknown without prior preparation.

            a)Develop an **initial concept** of the problem on the basis of information available at the outset.

            b)Generate **multiple hypotheses** as to the cause of the problem.

            c)Carry out an appropriate **inquiry** to attempt to establish the more likely cause.

            d)**Analyze** new data obtained through inquiry as it relates to the forming picture of the problem.

e)Add the new data that is thought to be significant, particularly in light of the hypotheses obtained, to a growing **problem synthesis.**

f)Continue this process, scanning for new information when stuck, creating new hypotheses as appropriate.

g)**Decide** at an appropriate point, despite inadequate or confusing data, on the most logical cause (hypothesis) and the appropriate treatment for the problem using criteria such as prevalence, seriousness, and treatability.

3)As the above process is going on, **learning issues** should be identified and recorded whenever knowledge or skills to understand appropriately or deal effectively with the problem or aspects of the problem are found to be lacking in the group.

4)At the completion of the problem encounter, when the group has committed itself to the probable mechanisms responsible for the problem and its management, the areas of needed learning through self-directed study are identified.

5)The appropriate **resources** for this learning are decided upon and also the time required for self-directed learning before the group returns to the problem.

C)Self-directed study is carried out by the individual members of the group for the time negotiated. During this, members of the group may decide to work together and consult, but there is no formal group meeting.

D)Follow-up session, following self-directed study, to complete work with the problem.

1)The learning resources used in self-study by each member of the group are critiqued and decisions are made about more appropriate resources in the future.

2)The problem is encountered again from the beginning, now that the group has learned all it thought it needed to learn in the first encounter with the problem. Problem solving with new knowledge, **app lying what has been learned in self-directed study**. The same stages are used as in B2 (above). As this is done, the group critiques its prior thinking. Further learning issues may surface and a new self-directed study period may be necessary before the next few steps are undertaken.

3)**Conscious integration of new learning**. The group verbalizes, systematizes and integrates the new information and skills gained.

4)**Evaluation** of problem solving skills, self-directed study skills and group support skills of each student is carried out in the group. The evaluation of each student is initiated by the student himself.

(For a more detailed discussion of this problem-based learning process in the small group, see Barrows and Tamblyn 1980 and Barrows 1985).

II.The **structure** of the Tutor's teaching process

A)Modeling the performance expected of the students through example by the tutor himself or through close coaching by the tutor to produce the desired performance in the students.

B)Guiding the students with challenges and comments at the metacognitive level.

C)Withdrawal from the group as the students begin to function effectively on their own, until the tutor is no longer necessary.

III.The **structure** of the group's interpersonal process

A)Initially, the students are courteous to each other and to the tutor and on their best behavior.

B)Eventually conflicts in personalities, behaviors and opinions invariably become apparent and may detract from the group's effectiveness.

C)Conflict resolution is followed by effective, high output by the group.

References

Barrows, H.S. *How to Design a Problem-based Learning Curriculum for the Preclinical Years.* 1985. New York: Springer-Verlag.

Barrows, H.S. A taxonomy of problem-based learning methods. *Journal of Medical Education* 20:481-486, 1986.

Barrows, H.S. *Simulated (Standardized) Patients and Other Human Simulations.* 1987. Chapel Hill, NC: Health Sciences Consortium.

Barrows, H.S., and Feltovich, P.J. The clinical reasoning process. *Journal of Medical Education* 21:86-91, 1987.

Barrows, H.S.; Myers, A.; Williams, R.G.; and Moticka, E.J. Large group problem-based learning: A possible solution for the '2 sigma problem. *Medical Teacher* 8(4):325-331, 1986.

Barrows, H.S., and Pickell, G.C. *Developing Clinical Problem-Solving Skills.* 1991. New York: W.W. Norton & Co.

Barrows, H.S., and Tamblyn, R. *Problem-Based Learning PS.* 1980. New York: Springer-Verlag.

Baron, J. Reflective thinking as a goal of education. *Intelligence* 5:291-309, 1981.

Brandsford, J.D., and Stein, B.S. *The Ideal Problem Solver.* 1984. New York: W.H. Freeman and Co.

Collins, A.; Brown, J.S.; and Newman, S.E. Cognitive Apprenticeship: Teaching the Craft of Reading, Writing, and Mathematics. In: Resnick, L.B. (Ed.) *Knowing, Learning, and Instruction. Essays in Honor of Robert Glaser.* (pp. 453-494). 1989. Hillsdale, NJ: Lawrence Erlbaum Associates.

Collins, A., and Stevens, A.R. In: Glaser, R. (Ed.) *Advances in Instructional Psychology,* Ch. 2, Goals and Strategies of Inquiry Teachers. 1983. Hillsdale, NJ: Lawrence Erlbaum Associates.

Distlehorst, L., and Barrows, H.S. The problem-based learning module: A new tool for problem-based, self-directed learning. *Journal of Medical Education* 57:486-488, 1982.

McCloskey, M.; Caramazza, A.; and Green, B. Curvilinear motion in the absence of external forces: Naive beliefs about the motion of objects. *Science* 210:1139-1141, 1980.

Schön, D.A. *The Reflective Practitioner: How Professionals Think in Action.* 1983. New York: Basic Books, Inc.